A start me up™ Book

Ancient Rome

By Dr. Ernst Künzl

Illustrated by Peter Klaucke

Tessloff Publishing

Preface

Throughout history many people have tried to build empires that controlled as much of the world as possible, but these empires rarely outlasted their founders. When Alexander the Great died, his empire fell apart. Rome and its generals were different. They conquered most of the known world and created an empire that lasted for centuries. Rome also became one of the major influences on the development of Medieval Europe and of modern Western states.

To people living in the United States, Rome may seem part of a past world not related to our present. If we look at our own government, however, we quickly see signs of Rome's influence on our world too: one of the centers of our government is the "capitol," where "senators" debate the laws of our "republic." The influence reaches deeper than names, however. If we look further we find elements of Roman law in our laws; we discover the tremendous influence of Latin—the language of ancient Rome—on the English language; we find the influence of

Roman architecture in our public buildings—and the list could go on and on.

Thanks to archaeologists who dig up Roman ruins and artifacts, and to literary scholars who study the writings of Roman authors, and to historians who study both writings and artifacts, we know a lot about this unique empire that grew up around the shores of the Mediterranean. Most of the artifacts now displayed in museums come from Rome's imperial age (31 BC-395 AD). Artifacts from the centuries of the Roman kings and the Roman republic (8th century BC to Julius Caesar's death in 44 BC) are much less common, but many important literary works from the republic have survived.

We know more about imperial Rome than we do about any of the other ancient cultures—more than we do about classical Athens, Babylon, Persia, or even Egypt. Drawing on the wealth of information available to us, this book answers many questions about Rome—from the early kings to the late empire.

Volume 8

PUBLISHERS: Tessloff Publishing, Quadrillion Media LLC

EDITOR: Alan Swensen

PICTURE SOURCES:

Aachener Domschatz: 9; AKG, Berlin: 5b, 6b, 32b; Architect of the Capitol: 4t; Courtesy of the General Assembly of Virginia: 4r; Bavaria Bildagentur, Gauting: 42; Bildarchiv Preussischer Kulturbesitz, Berlin: 8t, 24 (2), 31r, 45tl; Mark Bowen Photography, Cincinnati: 5t; dpa, Frankfurt: 6t; J. Felbermeyer: 23; Helga Lade Fotoagentur, Frankfurt: 32l; Prähistorische Staatssammlung, Munich: 38t; Rheinisches Landesmuseum, Bonn: 35; Römisch-Germanisches Zentralmuseum, Mainz: 8r, 9b, 12, 13, 15, 17, 19, 22, 25, 26, 31l, 33, 35 (3), 36r, 37, 38r, 39, 40, 45c, 47;

ILLUSTRATIONS: Peter Klaucke and Frank Kliemt

COPYRIGHT: © MCMXCVIII Tessloff Publishing, Burgschmietstrasse 2-4, 90419 Nuremberg, Germany
© MCMXCVIII Quadrillion Media LLC, 10105 East Via Linda Road, Suite 103-390, Scottsdale AZ 85258, USA

Visit us on the World Wide Web at http://www.quadrillionusa.com

Library of Congress Cataloging-in-Publication Data is available.

ISBN 1-58185-008-5

Printed in Belgium

Printing 10 9 8 7 6 5 4 3 2 1

Contents

Ancient Rome and the Young American Republic

This famous painting shows George Washington resigning his commission after the end of the Revolutionary War.

Who was Cincinnatus?

In December of 1783, after leading the American armies to victory over Great Britain, George Washington resigned his commission as general and returned to his home, Mount Vernon, to take up the life of a gentleman farmer once more. People around the world were amazed and called him a new "Cincinnatus."

What did they mean by this? When Washington resigned at the height of his power and success, he surprised powerful leaders in America and in Europe. They expected him to turn his military success into political power—

as Caesar had done in ancient Rome. By returning to private life and renouncing any claim to power, Washington reminded people of another ancient Roman, a man named Cincinnatus.

Lucius Quinctius Cincinnatus lived during the early years of the Roman republic—the form of government Romans developed when they freed themselves from their kings. In the republic citizens elected two "consuls" who jointly governed Rome for a one-year term. Elected legislative bodies also served the "republic." "Republic" comes from Latin *res* (thing, affair) *publica* (of the people)—the common good.

Ideally these elected officials served for a limited time and then

The sculptor Antoine Houdon depicted Washington as "Cincinnatus": he has hung his cloak and sword on the "fasces" and now holds the walking stick of a civilian.

With his hand resting on his plow, Cincinnatus surrenders the "fasces". The statue is located in Cincinnati, Ohio.

THE "FASCES"

were bundles of rods or sticks bound together with red thongs. They were symbols of a ruler's powers—representing the powers united in his office. A consul had 12 sticks in his bundle, a dictator had 24.

The engraving below shows Cincinnatus being called away from his plow to come to the aid of Rome's army.

returned to private life. When the republic was threatened with war, however, military leaders were given special powers and there was always the danger that they might not give up these powers after the danger had passed.

In 458 BC the Romans were at war with a neighboring people, the Aequi, and the war was going badly for the Romans. When the Aequi surrounded the armies of the consuls on Mount Algidus, the senate decided to appoint Cincinnatus "dictator" of Rome. This title didn't have a negative meaning back then, it was what they called the leader with special powers in a time of emergency.

According to the story, when messengers went to call Cincinnatus to serve the republic, they found him plowing the fields of his small farm. He immediately left his plow and went and led the army against the Aequi. He supposedly defeated them in one day. Once he saw that the republic was safe, he resigned and returned to his plow.

This was a model of republican virtue—a free citizen who served the republic when it needed him, but who did not aspire to become a professional politician or to gain power for his own personal profit. This was what many people in Washington's time saw in his resignation. He was so devoted to the idea of a free republic that he served when he was needed, and then freely returned the power to the republic and went back to private life.

Around the time of the Revolu-

> **How was republican Rome a model for the United States?**

tionary War many citizens of the American colonies were very interested in Rome. The kings and other nobles in Europe had been interested mostly in Rome's later history—when the republic had fallen and emperors began to rule Rome. These early Americans were more interested in the republic, however. It was a model for the kind of government they wanted: no one person or group had all the power.

The two consuls led the government, but other groups made the laws. There was an assembly of citizens—the *comitia*—and an assembly of the nobles—the senate. America's "Founding Fathers" not only followed this pattern in structuring the American constitution, they also took many names from Roman republican government: the "senate" and "senators," the "capitol," and the word "republic" itself. Many of the government buildings in Washington are also inspired by Roman architecture.

Some of the delegates who helped write the constitution believed the Roman republic had been too weak, however, and was not a good model—at least not without some modifications. The consuls only served for one year and this didn't give them time to get to know their office well enough. As a result their government wasn't always able to function as efficiently as it would with experienced rulers. This is one of the reasons why Julius Caesar was able to destroy the republic and pave the way for a Rome ruled by emperors.

A joint session of the Senate and the House of Representatives in the Capitol Building. Like the Roman republic the U.S. government has more than one legislative body.

What did the "Founding Fathers" think of imperial Rome?

The "Capitol" in Washington takes its name from the Capitoline Hill in Rome, and also draws on Roman architecture.

The delegates who took this position wanted the leader of the government to have more power than the consuls had had. They didn't want to create a tyrant like some of the Roman emperors, however, so they argued in favor of a strong central government with a president who would serve a term of four years. This was long enough to gain experience and then function effectively, but short enough to prevent the president from establishing himself permanently in power.

Those people who took this position clearly saw some value in imperial Rome's powerful central government. After all, Rome had managed to conquer most of the world known to them, and then preserve peace and stability in this huge empire for many centuries. North America was a vast land, and many early Americans expected it to become a great empire as well.

ROMAN NAMES were popular as "pen names" during the debate on the United States constitution. People used these names when they published pamphlets arguing for their ideas about the best constitution. One such author called himself "Brutus"—after the friend of Julius Caesar who killed Caesar to prevent him from destroying the republic. This author apparently felt that those who wanted a strong central government in the United States were going to destroy republican freedom as Caesar did.

The World Empire

What was the "mare nostrum?"

Even under its first emperor—Emperor Augustus—the Roman Empire controlled most of the world known to the Romans. From Italy, the Romans and their armies and fleets controlled all the coasts of the Mediterranean Sea. The Romans didn't always have a strong fleet of ships, however. In the First Punic War, in the years 264 and 241 BC, the Romans defeated the North African state of Carthage in naval battles. From that time on the Romans placed great emphasis on controlling the Mediterranean—not only for purposes of war, but also for the sake of keeping pirates and marauding Germanic tribes in check. They called the Mediterranean "mare nostrum"—our sea.

To inhabitants of the Mediterranean world at that time, the Roman Empire seemed even more colossal than it does to us. They were not aware of the existence of the Americas or Australia, or even of Scandinavian Europe. To the east they knew only of the Near East and parts of Central and Southern Asia—and this knowledge was probably limited to seafarers and geographers.

In the 2nd century AD the Roman Empire stretched from Scotland to Sudan and from the Caucasians to the Strait of Gibraltar. At the top of the map is the Capitoline she-wolf, the symbol of Rome.

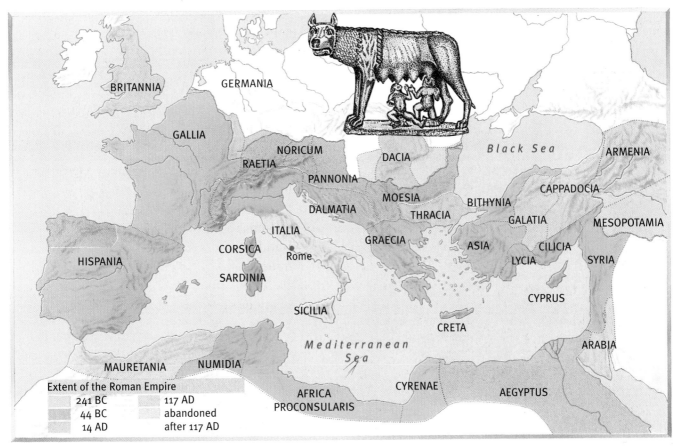

Extent of the Roman Empire

241 BC	117 AD
44 BC	abandoned
14 AD	after 117 AD

We can tell what the Romans

How did the Romans picture the world?

knew of the world from the world map of the astronomer and geographer Claudius Ptolemy, who lived in Alexandria in Egypt around 150 AD. One of his surviving works gives the co-ordinates of about 8,000 cities. Judging from his work, the Romans took notice only of those places that were of economic interest to them. Of Africa they knew only the part north of the equator; America and Australia were of course unknown to them. Northern Europe shows up in their records only as far as Denmark—although it would have been easy for them to explore all of Scandinavia.

The areas that interested them economically were primarily the Near East and Arabia, and they knew both quite well. Merchant caravans to Asia traveled along the "silk road" all the way to China. Seafaring merchants traveled more quickly to India and Ceylon (Sri Lanka). China, the empire of the Seres, appears at the very edge of the map. In Chinese works from the same period, the situation is exactly the opposite. From China's perspective, the states of the Near East, and along with them Rome, are located at the western edge of the world.

The Romans actually exported very few products, but they imported many things, particularly luxury goods. The rest of the world interested the Romans only if there were precious goods there that they could import: textiles—

The world map of the geographer and astronomer Ptolemy shows what Romans knew about the world in 150 AD.

above all Chinese silk, perfumes, drugs, precious stones, rare animals. If countries or regions weren't important for trade—Scandinavia, Northeastern Europe, Sub-Saharan Africa, and Northern Asia, for example—Rome didn't bother to send geographic expeditions there. The Romans were practical—voyages of discovery like those of Christopher Columbus would have had no attraction for them.

Emperor Theodosius on a silver plate from 388 AD.

Even when compared to large

How big was the Roman Empire?

modern nations Rome remains impressive. It is difficult to estimate the population of the empire since we lack the necessary records. For the first century AD we can only give a rough estimate of 50 to 80 million people in the entire empire—at most, about 1/4 of the present population of the United States. If we assume a population of 65 million, then the population density was about 73 per square mile—

WORLD MAPS existed already in the ancient world. People also knew that the world was round. They even made world globes, although they usually preferred flat maps for their representations of the Earth. These generally showed only a specific region—this way it wasn't so obvious that so many regions of the Earth were still unknown. The few globes that have been preserved or that we see depicted in reliefs are always maps of the heavens.

This brass celestial globe was made by a Roman craftsman between 150 and 220 AD. It is about 4 1/2 inches in diameter.

approximately the same as in the United States today.

Many people have speculated that the Roman aristocracy had a set plan to rule the world and that their military geniuses—Scipio, Marius, Sulla, Lucullus, Pompey—realized this plan in the course of the second and first centuries BC. It seems more likely, however, that each step in this process evolved out of the preceding one and was not part of a grand scheme. From a certain point on, it seems that Rome was simply drawn into whatever took place around the Mediterranean. At most one can say that Caesar had plans to conquer the world—as he demonstrated with his campaign in Asia Minor. In one point, however, there was obvious planning: Rome attempted to conquer the lands richest in raw materials—and succeeded in doing so.

How long did Rome last?

After the Roman Empire split in the year 395 AD, Germanic tribes soon conquered the entire Western Empire. The Eastern Empire continued to exist through the end of the Middle Ages. The Eastern Empire didn't end until 1453 when the Turks besieged and captured its capital—Byzantium (Constantinople)—and renamed it Istanbul.

For much of Europe the city of Rome continued to play an important role as the center of Christianity in the West. Ancient Rome never entirely disappeared as an ideal, however. After Charlemagne unified much of Germanic Europe

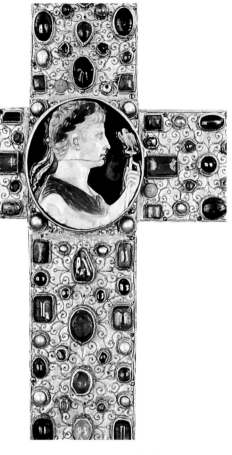

Emperor Augustus as triumphator in the cameo at the center of the medieval Lothar Cross in Aachen, Germany (10th century).

in the early Middle Ages, his empire soon became known as the "Holy Roman Empire of the German Nation." Its ruler wasn't called "German" emperor but rather "Roman" emperor. This empire lasted from the 10th century AD up until the beginning of the 19th century. The Italian Renaissance ("rebirth") signified in part an attempt to renew the glory of ancient Rome, and indeed, many of the ideals of the Renaissance were inspired by ancient Rome. If the empire inspired Europeans in the Middle Ages and Renaissance, it was republican Rome that inspired Europeans of the 18th century and the Enlightenment. The republican ideal inspired citizens of European colonies as well: Alexander Hamilton and Thomas Jefferson, for example.

The Military

Looking back at the civil wars of the late republic (133–31 BC), Emperor Augustus recognized that Rome needed a standing army it could count on. He divided the army into two groups: the legions, made up of soldiers who were Roman citizens, and the *auxilia*, made up of soldiers who could become citizens at the end of their period of service. The idea of a professional army was a new one, and with this army, Augustus had created a force that could help insure the stability of the huge Roman Empire.

In the centuries of the republic, all free Roman citizens were obligated to serve in the army. The legionaries of early Rome were proud to serve as free men. In this early period Rome's territories did not extend beyond the Italian Peninsula and an army of free citizens was adequate for such conditions. As Rome grew more powerful, however—from the time of their victory over Hannibal in 202 BC at the latest—there was little that happened in the Mediterranean region that didn't involve the Romans. The wars now being fought in more and more distant battlefields—against Spain, against the Gauls in what is now France, against tribes in what is now the Balkan region, and in Africa, Greece, Asia Minor, Syria, and Egypt—were too much for the old system in which the farmer-legionary returned to private life when the war was over. With both travel and battle, a citizen-soldier

When did Rome establish a professional army?

A legion marches along the Via Appia to a triumph in Rome.

MARCHING MUSIC was unknown to the Romans. The brass instruments of the troops were used to convey orders to the soldiers. The legions had the *cornu,* a curved horn; the *tuba,* a long trumpet-like horn; *lituus,* a short signal trumpet; and the *bucina,* another trumpet. When modern films show Roman legions marching into battle to the accompaniment of drums and trumpets, it's pure fiction.

The Roman auxiliaries also recruited archers from the Orient and barbarian warriors from the North.

might be away for several years, and by the time he returned home his fields were overgrown and his household in debt. Rome needed a professional army.

In the first century AD, the Roman army had about 30 legions. A legion consisted of 6,000 men. Including the auxiliary troops—the *auxilia*—there were about 250,000 soldiers ready for battle at any one time. There was also the fleet, the pretorian guard (the emperor's personal guard), and a special security force in the capital city. There were a few smaller units assigned to special tasks—reconnaissance, medical service, etc.

For about two hundred years after the reign of Augustus (31 BC–14 AD) the legions effectively carried out their tasks of securing the empire and even conquering new lands—Britain and the Rhineland, for example. In the course of the third century, however, the army had to be reorganized in order to cope with increasingly

Emperor Augustus above the officers of his legions: the legionary legate, a senatorial tribune, and five equestrian tribunes.

common border skirmishes with the Germanic tribes to the north and the Persians to the east. The legions were made smaller and hence more mobile, and a special mobile attack unit was created.

It was an ingenious move on the part of Augustus, to create the auxiliary troops—the *auxilia*. They were organized into "cohorts"—these were either pure infantry units or mixed infantry-cavalry units. There were also a few pure cavalry units—*alae*—such as the *ala secunda Flavia* at the outpost of Aalen on the border between the empire and the territories of the Germanic tribes.

Where did the auxilia come from?

In the auxilia, young men from Rome's provinces could find a good income and an opportunity to rise on the social ladder. The advantage of this arrangement for the Roman military forces was that they could capitalize on the special talents of the various peoples incorporated into the empire. Arab and North African horsemen served next to Syrian archers and Germanic cavalry, and soldiers with slings from the Balearic Islands complemented the Balkan infantry.

The Romans intentionally spread the auxilia throughout the empire in order to "uproot" them and "Romanize" them. Men from the eastern provinces served along the Rhine and in Britain, men from Northern Europe served in Asia Minor or in North Africa. The soldiers stationed in the Roman outpost of *Mogontiacum*—the present-day city of Mainz, in Germany—included horsemen from Parthia (Persia) and Arabia, and infantry and archers from Itruraea (present-day Lebanon and Jordan).

Soldiers in the auxilia received honorary discharge papers—the military diploma—after the completion of 25 years of service. This also brought with it Roman citizenship. The text of this diploma was a copy of the imperial decree that was displayed in Rome on a bronze plaque. In the long run, then, every veteran thus became a citizen.

What was a centurion?

As commander of a "century," the smallest tactical unit in the army, a centurion was the most important officer in battle. The centurions stood on the front line. The crests on their helmets ran from side to side rather than back to front—so their soldiers could see them better during battle. Every legion had 60 centurions, and they were clearly ranked from 1 to 60. At the top of the ranks was the first centurion of the first cohort—each legion consisted of 10 cohorts. He bore the title *primus pilus* and could be raised to the status of a nobleman. The centurions were probably among the best soldiers in all of history. They could also be distinguished from the other legionaries since they often wore the "muscled cuirass" of the staff officers. They also carried a cane as a symbol of their authority as commanders.

Honorable discharge (military diploma) cast in bronze. This conferred citizenship on veterans of the auxiliaries after they completed 25 years of service.

Centurion in scale armor with a transverse (side to side, not back to front) crested helmet, greaves, and the cane as symbol of his authority. Unlike the legionary, the centurion wore his sword on the left side.

PLATE ARMOR such as that worn by the legionary (pictured on the right) was introduced as part of Emperor Augustus' military reforms. It was a Roman innovation and offered good protection and was also easy to repair.

was extremely hard. Only those who held up well under the four months of training were accepted into the legion. Driven by their centurion, the recruits practiced marching in step and learned to endure long marches while carrying heavy packs. Training with weapons didn't begin until the men were already in good physical condition.

How good were Roman weapons?

The Romans were always very practical. A typical example of this are the weapons of the Roman legionaries in the first century BC. Of all their different weapons there was probably only one that was a true Roman invention: plate armor. All the rest were adopted from others: helmets from the Etruscans and Celts; armor from the Celts and Greeks; spears, daggers, and swords from the Iberians. The Romans didn't really care where a thing came from—all that mattered was that it worked.

A legionary wore a helmet (*galea*) with a neckguard and cheekpieces and armor—chain mail (*lorica hamata*), for example. He carried a shield (*scutum*) and two spears (*pilum*) as well as a sword (*gladius*). A centurion wore all of this plus greaves (shin armor) and a helmet with a side-to-side crest, a commander's staff, and many medals. The practice of displaying medals on a band across the chest is yet another Roman invention.

A legionary from the time of Augustus—around the time of Jesus' birth—wore his short gladius on his right hip since his left hip had to support a heavy shield. The skirt of metal-trimmed leather flaps—there were apparently many different forms of this skirt—didn't have much practical use and probably served as decoration.

Legionary of the early empire with marching gear.

In the first century AD the army introduced articulated plate armor made from plates of metal joined together. While on the march a legionary carried a heavy pack containing weapons, tools, cooking utensils, provisions, and perhaps a

The tombstone of the centurion Marcus Caelius, who fell in the battle against the Germans in 9 AD. It was found near Xanten, Germany.

few personal effects. All together this usually weighed more than 60 pounds.

Roman auxiliary cavalry of the first century AD was somewhat differently armed than the legionaries. Since the short gladius was useless to a soldier on a horse, the cavalry used long swords and lances. They also used a lighter shield. The helmets of the riders were often very imaginatively decorated. The infantry among the auxiliary troops was likewise armed with long swords and lances and thus easily distinguished from legionaries.

A legionary in the 1st century AD wore armor and a helmet, and carried a shield, javelin, sword, and dagger.

symbols that helped the soldiers maintain their orientation during battle. These standards were also considered sacred—especially the legionary golden eagle. Each legion also had its own specific emblem. For example, the emblems of two of the legions stationed in Britain were pegasus (the winged horse) for the 2nd legion "Augusta" and a boar for the 20th legion "Valeria Victrix." Instruments like the *tuba* (a long trumpet-like instrument) and *cornu* (something like a French horn) weren't used to create music but rather to give signals.

In the course of the empire the armaments changed. Legionaries from the time around 200 AD and after now carried a long sword (*spatha*) and a lance (*hasta*) as the auxiliaries had done—since they now had to fight against mounted troops more and more frequently. They hung their swords from a shoulder strap and not from their belt. Helmets were now designed solely for protection and probably made it hard to move quickly.

PARTHIAN ARMED HORSE-MEN soundly defeated the Romans in battle in 53 BC. The Romans had never seen this form of heavily armed cavalry. In the 2nd century AD the Romans themselves created their own troops of this type, with both man and horse entirely covered in scale or plate armor.

What was the battle strategy of the legionaries?

At the beginning of a battle the legionaries marched out in tight rows and each hurled his *pilum*—a spear with a long, thin iron tip. The tips of the spears usually lodged in the shields of the enemies and left them without cover. In the hand combat that followed, the Roman legionaries covered themselves with long shields and pushed forward, stabbing their enemies with their short swords (*gladius*). This combat technique is known as the "pilum-gladius" strategy.

Roman military standards—the *signa*—were visual command

What were riding tournaments for?

Occasionally the Roman cavalry held riding displays or competitions. They were concerned as much with skillful riding as with tournament-like combat. The two parties wore helmets with face guards, parade armor, and carried colorful shields. The horses were equipped with forehead armor, eye guards, and a breast shield. Parade weapons are some of the most artful products of Roman metalwork.

Roman cavalry of the 1st century AD during an attack. They didn't have stirrups back then.

Legionaries in battle: the javelin (pilum) hinders the opponent, and the short sword (gladius) completes the attack.

Riding tournaments were introduced as part of Augustus' military reforms. The oldest artifacts from such games stem from this time. On the battlefield where Germanic tribes defeated the Roman general Varus and at a Roman camp in

The cap from the pole of a dragon flag: Rome adopted this Asiatic field symbol for its cavalry.

Germany, archaeologists found iron face masks from parade helmets.

Roman helmets often bore the image of the Macedonian king Alexander the Great. His victory over the Persians and his conquests in Asia and India had made him the ideal of many Roman generals and emperors.

In the army Latin was the customary language both for military commands and for everyday use, although Greek was occasionally spoken in the Eastern parts of the empire. As the experiences of soldiers in the French Foreign Legion have demonstrated, soldiers often learned the language of the area they were stationed in quite quickly.

Auxiliary troops served for 25 years. Anyone who survived this long and often dangerous time became a Roman citizen. Such soldier-citizens continued to speak Latin, and for their children it was not terribly important that they had previously been Britons, Teutons, Thracians, or Syrians. The German tribal leader Arminius was a Roman citizen as was the Jew Saul—later Paul, one of the key figures in early Christianity. The Romans didn't care whether the

What did the army mean to new citizens of Rome?

new citizens were Teutons, Celts, Africans, or Arabs. To persecute an entire people or religious group solely because of racial differences was for the most part foreign to Rome. They preferred to integrate the best inhabitants of the provinces into the empire. This practice made the Roman Empire attractive to many of those they conquered and helps to explain how Rome was able to prosper for so long. In 248 AD, when the city of Rome celebrated 1,000th anniversary of its founding, its emperor was an Arab—Philippus Arabs!

In tournaments of the Roman cavalry soldiers wore ornate parade armor.

THE "TURTLE" TACTIC was used by Romans when they were attacked. They gathered into a square and the outermost soldiers held their shields out from the group to form a protective band. The others formed a shell over their heads with the remaining shields.

The borders of the empire that were most heavily guarded were Britain, the Rhine and Danube rivers, and the Asian borders.

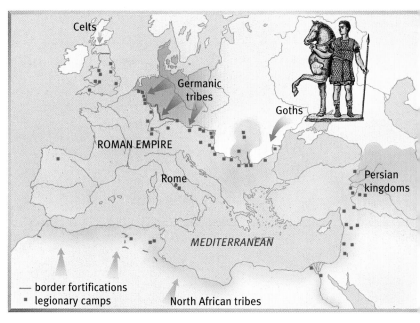

Celts
Germanic tribes
Goths
ROMAN EMPIRE
Rome
Persian kingdoms
MEDITERRANEAN

— border fortifications
■ legionary camps

North African tribes

The imperial borders weren't all equally well guarded. Heavy concentrations of troops were kept in Britain, on the northern border along the Rhine and Danube rivers, and on the eastern border along the Euphrates River. In North Africa the military was concentrated in the west—Morocco, Algeria, and Tunisia. In other words, an army of around 250,000 men had to secure the enormous stretches of land that made up the empire.

The border running between the Rhine and the Danube was one of the most heavily defended zones in the empire. After plans to extend the empire all the way to the Elbe River failed, the Romans gradually began to improve connections between the Rhine and the Danube and at the same time to push Rome's border northward from Mainz. The result was the limes in Upper Germany. It lasted only a hundred years or so, however, and then the Romans abandoned the right bank of the Rhine.

Emperor Hadrian had a wall built along the limes in northern Britain. Construction began in 122 AD. The wall was built just south of the present border between England and Scotland. It is about 73 miles long, 10 feet thick, and was once 15 to 20 feet high. In front of the wall was a dry moat and in front of this an embankment. At one-mile intervals the Romans built small forts—a Roman mile is somewhat shorter than our present-day mile. Between one "fortlet" and the next there were two watchtowers about 1,600 feet apart. Soldiers could see from one tower to the next and communicate with flag and horn signals.

ARMOR was often very elaborate, like the cavalry helmet shown below. It was made according to a Greek model and decorated with reliefs, an eagle, and a feather crest.

Horseman's helmet from Theilenhofen in Bavaria (3rd century AD).

What was the limes?

The word *limes* refers both to a continuous border line or wall, and to the border zones that zigzagged across the landscape. Neither Hadrian's Wall in northern England, nor the Upper German palisade with its mounds and moats, nor the Rhaetian wall in present-day southern Germany were actually border fortifications. Unlike the Great Wall of China, these lines could not be defended easily. When an attack occurred, the troops had to rush to the border to face and destroy the enemy that was attempting to enter the empire.

Camps like *Novaesium* on the

How large were Rome's military camps?

Rhine measured more than 1,300 by 1,900 feet—an area of about 60 acres. A legion had 10 cohorts, and the first and best cohort had twice as many men as the others. Each cohort had 6 centurions. In addition to this there were 6 military tribunes from among the Roman nobles: five from the equestrian order and one from the senatorial order. The commander of the legion was also from the senatorial order. Only enlisted men and centurions were professional soldiers, however. Tribunes and commanders served as part of a normal political career. Including cavalry, special troops, and sanitary personnel, a legion at full strength had more than 6,000 men.

The fortifications of auxiliary troops were constructed like little legion encampments—a bit more than 400 by 500 feet—roughly

5 acres. Archaeological finds along the limes are an important source of our knowledge about the Roman military system.

Between the Rhine and Wuerttemberg, the Upper German limes was a palisade fence with a dry moat, embankment, and watchtowers.

Caesar's costly and extended

Were the Romans masters of siege warfare?

sieges are well known—in Burgundy, for example, or in Judea during the Jewish War around 70 AD, when Titus conquered Jerusalem. After the fall of Jerusalem in 70 AD, the Romans laid siege to the fortress of Masada on the Dead Sea in 72–73 AD. You can still see the impressive remains of the Roman camp and of the ramp that the Roman general Flavius Silva had his soldiers build. The wall that encircled the Masada was over 11,000 feet long. The wall the Romans

The military border (limes) along the Rhine and Danube was one of the most heavily manned military zones in the empire.

MILITARY CAMPS often developed into real cities. The simple wooden structures were replaced by stone buildings and the townspeople built fountains, water lines, and streets. They also began farming land around the camp. Many people settled around the camps to buy products from the camps or offer their own services to the camp. Gradually the camp grew into a large city. The city of Cologne (*Colonia*) in Germany developed from a military camp.

LOWER GERMANY

FREE GERMANY

Cologne

Rheinbrohl

Limes

Mainz

Main

Rhine

Limes

Regensburg

UPPER GERMANY

Danube

ROMAN EMPIRE

⌇⌇⌇ Palisade
⌇⌇⌇ Wall

DEAD SEA

■ Jewish Fortification
■ Roman Fortification

Storage Buildings

Camps

Administration

Herod's Terraced Palace

Living Quarters

Villas

Synagogue

Western Palace

Camp

Gate

Camp

Roman Storm Ramp

Camp

Main Camp of Flavius Silva

Camp

Camp

Roman Siege Wall (about 11,000 feet long)

After the fall of Jerusalem in 70 AD, the Romans besieged the fortress of Masada on the Dead Sea. They built a wall around it that was more than 2 miles long.

built to enclose the fortress of Numantia (in present-day Spain) in 135–134 BC was more than 5 miles long and contained seven Roman camps of different sizes.

It was rare that the Romans did not succeed in capturing a fortress they besieged. In the case of the Masada, the Romans could have simply starved their enemy out—in a very unwarlike manner and without losses. This didn't agree with their military philosophy, however. A war won without battle was not honorable. So they built a ramp—an unimaginably difficult task—and captured the Masada in May of 73 AD, long after the official war had ended. When the soldiers finally penetrated the fortification, none of its occupants were alive—they had taken their own lives so they wouldn't fall into Roman hands.

Reconstruction of a Roman fort. There were barracks (1), legionary headquarters (2), commander's quarters (3), storehouses (4), stables (5), and a hospital (6).

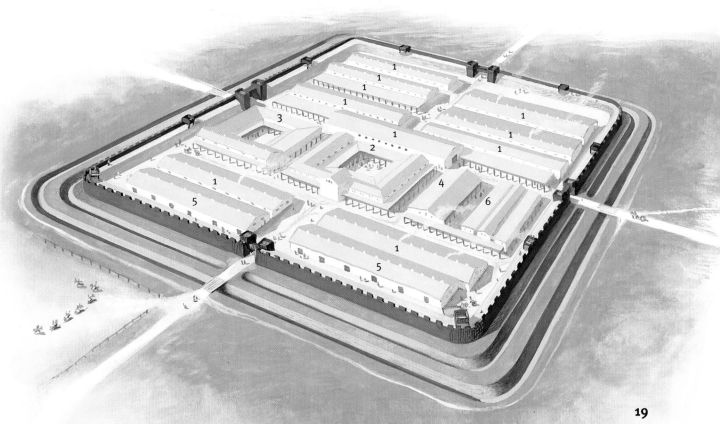

What was the role of the fleet?

The Roman republic laid the foundation for a world-wide empire when it built its own fleet. Roman ships became the ruling force in the Mediterranean. With this fleet the Romans decisively defeated their greatest rival—the city of Carthage on the northern coast of Africa—in 269 and 241 BC.

The age of the great sea battles was over by the time of the empire. The last one took place in 31 BC when Augustus defeated Cleopatra and Mark Anthony at Actium in western Greece. This naval battle marked the beginning of Augustus' rule and thus of imperial Rome. The imperial fleet served to secure border areas and also the shipping routes Rome needed for the import of grain and other goods. Since the Mediterranean had become an inland sea for Rome, pirates were among their main enemies at sea.

The Romans were masters of siege warfare. This picture shows the storming of Jerusalem under Titus in the year 70 AD.

PIRATES were a serious danger for Roman merchant ships. They seized the ships, stole the freight, and killed the crew or sold them into slavery. Not until 67 BC did the Roman fleet—under Pompey—succeed in freeing the Mediterranean of pirates.

Roman warships had a ram on the bow end, beneath the water level, and a movable boarding bridge or gangplank—the corvus.

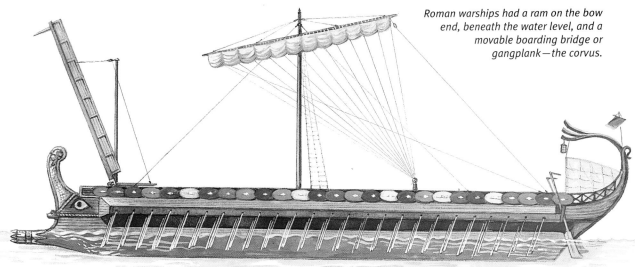

THE FLEET was especially important in the unsecured northern regions of the empire. When the province of Gaul was occupied and plundered by Germans in 275–277 AD, the Romans were still able to hold their bases along the Rhine thanks to their quick warships. They also sunk many of the German transports carrying plunder.

What kinds of ships did Rome have?

The slaves who rowed in the galleys of the Roman warships in "Ben Hur" give us a false impression of Roman practices. It was not common to condemn someone "to the galleys" in the ancient world. The oarsmen on Roman ships were free sailors and not slaves.

The typical Roman warship in the late republic and early empire was built for ramming enemy ships and had a ramming post below water level on its front end. Other important uses of the ships were for transporting infantry to board enemy ships and for transporting artillery towers. One of their great successes was a large gangplank—its nickname was the *corvus* ("raven" or "crow")—that could be lowered onto an enemy ship for boarding.

The warships of the Romans were never very large, but during the 3rd and 4th centuries AD they became even trimmer and more maneuverable. Wartime experiences in Germania in the north and on rivers such as the Rhine and Thames contributed to the development of a small but speedy warship in late antiquity.

1. 2. 3. 4.

Kings, Consuls, and Emperors

During Rome's early period—

Who were the kings of the early period?

from its founding in 753 BC until 510 BC—it was ruled by kings. The *fasti triumphales*—inscriptions in stone that record year by year the triumphs celebrated—list Rome's founder, Romulus, as the first triumphator in Roman history and describe him as King Romulus, the son of Mars, the god of war.

Already by the time of the late republic many Romans considered the stories about the early kings of Rome to be mostly legends from ancient times. Between 753 and approximately 510 BC, Rome had seven kings, and Romulus was the first. Between 600 and 510 BC Etruscan kings ruled in Rome: Tarquinius Priscus, Servius Tullius, and Tarquinius Superbus (*superbus* means "the proud").

Around the year 510 BC the Roman aristocrats (patricians) rebelled against the Etruscan kings.

They drove Tarquinius Superbus from his throne and created a government of officers (magistrates) elected on a yearly basis: for one year at a time, two consuls of equal authority led the commonwealth or *res publica* (literally: *res* = thing or affair; *publica* = of the people). The Roman republic was not a democracy in the modern sense, however. All members of the upper classes—and later all citizens—could participate in government, but there were slaves and others who had no voice in government.

The beginnings of Roman law date back to 450 BC, when the senate passed a legal code known as the Twelve Tables Law—this was a set of laws that were inscribed on 12 tablets and set up in the forum. Thus the Roman republic laid the cornerstone for a legal system that was famous even in antiquity. Even today modern students of law still study the Roman legal system since it strongly influenced our modern legislation.

In Rome you could tell what class people belonged to by the clothes they wore.

THE RULING CLASS in Rome consisted of the senators and the imperial family. The senators were distinguished by a toga with a purple stripe (above left). Titus, as supreme commander (above right), wears a general's cloak, a muscled cuirass, and fur boots. Emperor Vespasian (69–79) wears a white triumphal garment with gold trim and a gold wreath set with precious stones.

Rulers of the Roman Empire: 1. Caesar, 2. Augustus, 3. Nero, 4. Trajan, 5. Commodus.

IN TIMES OF CRISIS the republic created a special office: the dictator. The senate elected a dictator in times of war and gave him complete control for a limited time. The term of office for a dictator was limited to six months. This corresponded to the "war season" in antiquity—they didn't usually fight during the winter months. This office disappeared in the imperial era.

When did Rome become a world power?

In the course of the 5th and 4th centuries BC Rome expanded its rule over its immediate neighbors and over large parts of central Italy. By 266 BC it had become the most important power on the Italian peninsula. In 202 BC, two generations and two wars later—wars against the Carthaginians or "Punians" (hence, "Punic Wars")—Rome defeated the Carthaginian general Hannibal at Zama in Tunisia and established itself as the greatest power in the Mediterranean region—and thus the greatest power in the world as they knew it.

The two consuls elected by the aristocracy held office for one year at a time. This was often a disadvantage during times of war. In 216 BC in the battle at Cannae in the south of Italy, Hannibal succeeded in defeating two consuls and their eight legions because the consuls hadn't followed the effective delaying tactic practiced by one of their predecessors. This defeat was the worst catastrophe in Roman history. In the course of the battle Rome lost 70,000 soldiers.

Rome found itself with a governmental crisis. The republic was governed by two consuls and a number of other high government officials—the praetors, aediles, censors, and plebeian (people's) tribunes. This form of government was appropriate for a city-state of moderate size, but not for a vast territory that by the 2nd century BC already included provinces in Spain, North Africa, southern France, Greece, and Asia Minor.

How did the hundred years of civil war affect Rome?

The larger the Roman republic became, the greater the internal problems it had to confront. Civil wars broke out in Rome and lasted for more than 100 years—from 133 until 31 BC.

Rome had become rich. At the same time, there were also many great military leaders like Sulla, Pompey, and Caesar, who were no longer content to abide by the constitution of the republic. Mismanagement of the provinces had become a perpetual scandal, and the provincial governors exploited the situation instead of trying to control it. The peasantry and the proletarian population grew poorer and poorer. The legions

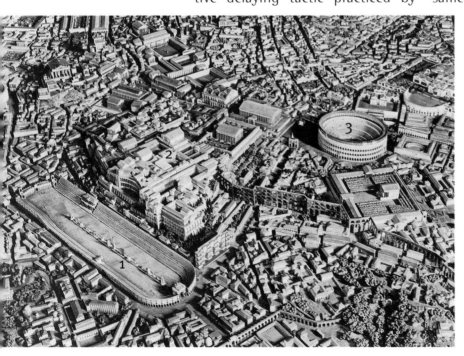

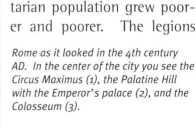

Rome as it looked in the 4th century AD. In the center of the city you see the Circus Maximus (1), the Palatine Hill with the Emperor's palace (2), and the Colosseum (3).

increasingly shifted their loyalty from the republic to their individual commanders. All of this led to a situation that fostered the transformation from republic to empire. Caesar was on the verge of becoming Rome's first emperor. He was murdered in 44 BC before this could happen, but his name survived into the modern world as the title of rulers over large empires: "Kaiser" (German) and "Tsar" (Russian).

Augustus learned from Caesar's mistakes and attempted to preserve at least the impression that he meant to preserve the republic. The two consuls were elected each year, and the senate continued to exist as always.

Why was Augustus an emperor without a title?

There was one very important change, however. Augustus divided the empire into provinces that were ruled by the emperor and provinces that were ruled by the senate. Each year Augustus had the army swear an oath of allegiance recognizing his authority (*imperium*) as highest military commander. He also created a standing army to replace the militia of citizens and stationed the new legions only in imperial provinces. He was thus automatically the most powerful force in the empire. On the authority of the people's tribune he was declared "inviolable in life and limb." He had his own financial administration and controlled the most important border provinces. He could therefore afford to have himself called simply "princeps"— the "first" in the state. This word is the root of our words "prince" and "principality." Augustus' residence on the Palatine Hill in Rome and his private life were decidedly modest. The Romans had become accustomed to the pomp of expanding empires, but to see it in a single ruler would have tempted them to compare his rule with that of more autocratic Greek-style kings.

This bust depicts the first emperor, Augustus (31 BC–14 AD), with an oak wreath, as the "renewer of the city."

"BEST OF EMPERORS"— *Optimus Princeps*—was the title that Roman historians gave to Trajan, who was emperor from 98–117 AD.

MARBLE BUSTS AND COIN FACES give us a picture of many of the Roman emperors, but they weren't realistic, photo-like images. They were meant to give the public a specific image of the emperor. The emperor himself decided how he would be portrayed.

Statues of Roman politicians were meant to portray their character. This bust is of Gaius Julius Caesar (100–44 BC).

This portable gold bust of emperor Marcus Aurelius (161–180 AD) could be carried from place to place and represented imperial authority at trials and ceremonies.

executed Christians for the entertainment of spectators. In the provinces, however, he was a rather popular ruler. After an alleged conspiracy against him, the town of Mainz in Upper Germany (*Germania Superior*) set up a large column dedicated to his prosperity. After his suicide the rumor circulated in several of the provinces that he was still alive and would return.

Many of the emperors were more or less megalomaniacal psychopaths—for example, Caligula (37–41 AD), Domitian (81–97 AD), Commodus (180–192 AD), and Caracalla (212–217 AD). Others, however, such as Vespasian (69–71 AD), Titus (79–81 AD), Trajan (98–117 AD), and Marcus Aurelius (161–180 AD) were praised as model rulers even generations later. Trajan in particular was considered to be the greatest emperor of all. If an emperor was unusually bad, the Romans erased all reminders of him. After the deaths of Nero and Commodus, the Romans obliterated their names from all public inscriptions and toppled and destroyed all statues of them.

THE EMPERORSHIP was so firmly established after the first two emperors—Augustus and Tiberius—that even Caligula's reign of terror didn't shake it. Reports say he condemned countless innocent people to do hard labor in mines or to fight animals in the arena. After his death the senate ordered all images of him destroyed.

Did all the emperors suffer from megalomania?

We sometimes associate the name Caesar or the title "Emperor of Rome" with the idea of a ruler with an abnormally intense desire for power and grandeur. The contemporaries of the various Roman emperors didn't necessarily share this view. The Roman historian Tacitus strongly criticized Tiberius (14–37 AD), the successor of Emperor Augustus, but Tiberius was nevertheless a very competent military commander. Nero (54–68 AD) set fire to Rome, killed his mother, and tortured and

How did imperial propaganda function?

Try to imagine for a moment what it would have been like when one emperor died and another succeeded him—for example, when Claudius succeeded Caligula as emperor in 41 AD. In Rome many knew the new emperor personally, though of course not everyone did. They probably became familiar with him most quickly from his image on

Apotheosis (becoming a god) of Emperor Antoninus Pius (138–161) and his wife Faustina from a large relief in Rome.

newly minted coins. The inscriptions on the coins were also a tried and proven means of securing his authority—the coin displayed the emperor's various titles in addition to his image and other flattering statements. The emperor also had statues of himself made, in both bronze and marble, and set up throughout the empire. On huge state monuments the emperor was honored both in direct depictions of his life and deeds or in allegorical illustrations—"historical reliefs."

What was the "triumph"?

The triumph—today we would say "triumphal procession"— was the high point in the career of any Roman commander. The triumph was a celebration in honor of Jupiter, but also a festival that promised good fortune for the entire state. The victorious commander, the triumphator, marched from the Field of Mars up to the Capitoline Hill—a triumphal route more than two miles long. Here the spoils of war were displayed and prisoners were executed. The celebration ended at the Capitol—the citadel on the Capitoline Hill. Here they made sacrifices to Jupiter.

From the year 71 AD on, imperial Rome reserved the triumphal procession for emperors alone, and the emperors increasingly wore the symbols of a triumphator—purple toga, golden wreath, and eagle scepter—as their normal attire. The emperor now saw himself as an eternal triumphator.

What did "pax Romana" mean?

Despite set backs and defeats, the Roman Empire endured and senatorial rule never returned. Even before the reign of Augustus the Roman republic had never been a democracy in the modern sense, but rather a state led by the nobility.

THE OVATIO, which gave us the word "ovation," was a kind of substitute for the triumphal procession. Like the triumph, the *ovatio* had to be approved by the senate. It was more modest than the triumph, however. The commander entered the city on foot, the wreaths were of myrtle and not of laurel, and the celebration was not so grand.

MARCELLUS, victor over Syracuse in 212 BC, insisted that Rome grant him only the ovatio. He thus showed himself in a decidedly modest light. Later, however, he celebrated a triumph on the Alban Mount.

The triumphal procession of Titus and Vespasian after their victory over the Jews in 71 AD. The course of the triumph ran from the forum to the Capitoline Hill and the temple of Jupiter located there.

Rome saw it as its task in the world to preserve peace, justice, and order among the peoples under its rule. This wasn't an easy task, since the empire included many, many different peoples—from Britons to Egyptians, from Iberians to Syrians. By enforcing this Roman peace—pax Romana—Rome meant to provide the necessary basis for a prosperous empire.

Augustus brought peace and prosperity to his empire and established the policy of pax Romana. This policy interrupted the endless wars that again and again spread ruin throughout the known world. This "Augustan" peace outlived the emperor and in time was seen as the essence of imperial rule.

Failures were unable to diminish the fascination that emanated from the Roman Empire. Rome remained the ideal for rulers in Europe and elsewhere: German emperors in the Middle Ages, Emperor Napoleon, the Fascist dictator Mussolini, and Russia's Tsars. The United States constitution has features reminiscent of the Roman principate—for example, the strong position granted to the president.

From Village to World Capital

Long before 753 BC—according to legend the date Rome was founded—there were settlements on the east side of the Tiber River and on most of the seven hills of Rome. Then in the 8th century BC, under the leadership of the mythical twins Romulus and Remus—sons of the god Mars—the settlers united. This was the birth of the city of Rome, *Urbs Roma*. Rome quickly developed into a large city, since there was an important trade route that crossed the river south of the Tiber island.

The Rome of the Etruscan kings—in the 6th century BC—was already an impressive city. From the 3rd century on, peasants who had fallen on hard times fled into the city in ever increasing numbers and swelled the urban proletariat. Poorly constructed multi-story tenement housing dominated some quarters of Rome. There are reports of deaths and injuries caused when buildings collapsed. Despite aqueducts—bridge-like structures that channeled water into the city—and new, paved streets that connected the lands ruled by Rome, life cannot have been easy in late republican Rome. Frequent gladiator fights, chariot races, triumphal and religious processions, and festivals were politically necessary—they distracted the city's poor from their misery. Chariot races were especially popular among the Romans. They were held on a long oval track—the Circus.

During the empire sport facilities and places of entertainment stand out in particular: Circus Flaminius in the south part of the

Rome at the time of its founding: hilltop settlements in the 8th century BC probably looked something like this. In later years the Romans displayed a hut from early times on the Palatine Hill. It was supposed to have been the home of the city's founder, Romulus.

CHARIOT RACES were probably adopted from the Greeks and were very popular among the commoners. At the Circus you could meet friends, bet on horses, and cheer them on with loud shouting. There were many teams and their fans were bitter opponents. The races often ended in brawls.

Rome was one huge pedestrian zone. The streets were packed and the swarm of people and the traffic were very loud.

Field of Mars; Circus Maximus in the city center (it held 250,000 spectators), the playing field (*stadium*) of Emperor Domitian in the north part of the Field of Mars; the Colosseum (the Flavian amphitheater) in the city center, and the gigantic baths, spread throughout the whole city—the *thermae* of Agrippa, Nero, Titus, Trajan, Caracalla, Diocletian, and other wealthy sponsors. The large theaters in the south part of the Field of Mars weren't dramatic stages. They offered revues or operetta-like entertainment.

When Nero burned Rome in 64 AD it wasn't the first time Rome had burned—though certainly one of the most destructive. In the republic, because of irresponsible building practices—buildings with too many stories too lightly built—there was a constant danger of fire. When Augustus boasted that he had turned Rome into a marble city he was speaking only of temples and public buildings. The houses of the poor were still built of wood and bricks. Nero was accused of burning Rome simply so he could rebuild it according to his own plans, more splendid than before. He actually concentrated his efforts on his palace—a complex of buildings in the center of the city. His successors undid most of his building projects. The Colosseum stands on the site of a pond in the gardens belonging to the "Golden House" (*domus aurea*), as Nero's palace was called.

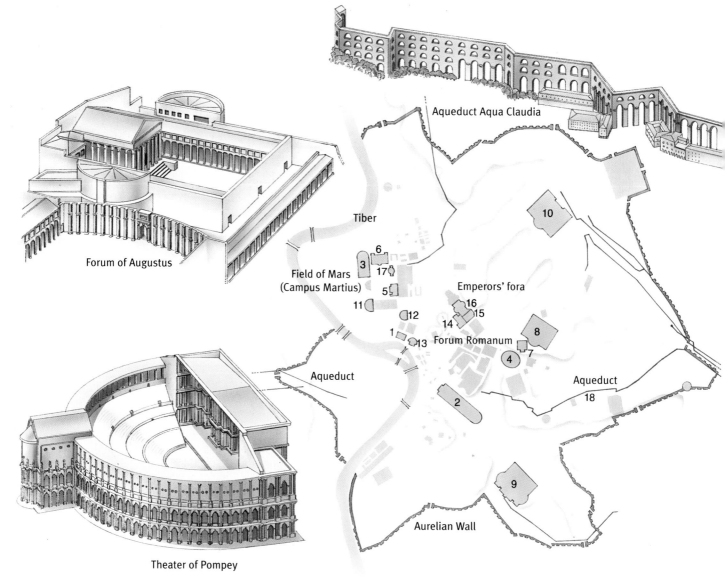

Forum of Augustus

Aqueduct Aqua Claudia

Tiber

6
3 17
5
11

Field of Mars
(Campus Martius)

12
1
13

10

Emperors' fora

16
15
14

Forum Romanum

8
7
4

2

Aqueduct

9

Aqueduct
18

Aurelian Wall

Theater of Pompey

Did Rome practice city planning?

Rome was the political center of the republic, and the Roman Forum (*forum Romanum*) was the center of Rome. This large open square in the center of the city served as a gathering place for the people. In the course of many building projects, Augustus and his successors made it increasingly more symmetrical and presented it as one of the most revered sites in Roman history—when the public assembly of the republic had long been a thing of the past. In general, the Romans of both the republic and the empire had a strong preference for plazas and temples that were symmetrically arranged. In this they were following Greek models. The so-called "emperors' fora" (*fora* = plural of *forum*), especially those of Caesar, Augustus, and Trajan, were magnificent plazas with arcades on the sides and a large temple in the middle.

Aside from the grand plazas and buildings in the center of the city, Rome continued to have problems with the city's buildings. Most of the streets were much too narrow. Still, by the 2nd century there were solidly built multi-story houses in the center of the city. In the outlying districts of the city—Augustus had divided the city into 14 dis-

Rome in the time of the empire:
1) Portico of Octavia
2) Circus Maximus (largest racing arena)
3) Domitian's Stadium
4) Colosseum (the Flavian amphitheater)
5) Baths of Agrippa
6) Baths of Nero
7) Baths of Titus
8) Baths of Trajan
9) Baths of Caracalla
10) Baths of Diocletian
11) Theater of Pompey
12) Theater of Balbus
13) Theater of Marcellus
14) Forum of Julius Caesar
15) Forum of Augustus
16) Forum of Trajan
17) Pantheon
18) Aqueduct of Claudius

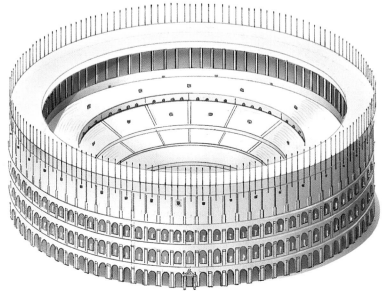

Colosseum

Many of Rome's buildings—the temples, the arcades surrounding the plazas, the amphitheaters, aqueducts, and pump houses—had magnificent facades. The Romans were also masters in the design of interior spaces. The dome of the Pantheon, a temple built by Emperor Hadrian to honor all of the gods, appears very modest from the outside but from the inside it is the most beautiful dome in ancient architecture—along with the Hagia Sophia in Constantinople (Istanbul). The vaults in Roman baths arched over warm and cold bathing areas of huge dimensions and overwhelming splendor. This was also true of the imperial palaces on the Palatine, one of the seven hills

THE STADIUM erected by Emperor Domitian (81–96 AD) on the Field of Mars (3 on the map on page 30) still lends its character to that part of the city. The form of this structure

is reflected in the layout of one of the most beautiful plazas in Rome, the Piazza Navona. Bernini's famous Fountain of the Four Rivers dominates the center of the plaza.

tricts—life must have had a very small-town flavor in many cases. Since there was no public transportation many people probably never left their quarter of the city.

The city walls of Rome—parts of these walls are still standing today—were built under Emperor Aurelianus (270–275). Since the 4th century BC Rome had not needed walls any more. For a long time it was virtually unfortified. Now the Teutons were once again threatening the city, however. But even the Aurelian walls weren't able to prevent enemies—Alarich and the Western Goths—from capturing Rome in 410 AD. This was the first time since the attack of the Gauls in 377 BC that the city had been taken.

The Pantheon in Rome was a temple for all the gods. It is one of the most beautiful domed buildings of all times.

Rome was built on—it unfolded its riches inside more than outside.

Versatile, functional structures illustrate the genius of Roman architecture. In some cases, Roman bridges have lasted into our times. Roman aqueducts supplied cities with fresh water in such quantities and of such a quality that until recently, even modern countries had nothing that could compare. The baths are also very famous, and not only those of the capital city but those of other Roman cities as well. Nearly every North

Pont-du-Gard aqueduct in France was a major architectural achievement. It served both as a water line and as a bridge.

African city of moderate size had more public baths per capita than a big city in modern Europe, where public baths were still common in recent times. The city of Timgad in Algeria had nine thermae, yet its center was the size of a legion's camp and had about 10,000 inhabitants. The hall where market and court were held—the *basilica*—became the model for church interiors from late antiquity to the Middle Ages.

In keeping with Rome's practical way of thinking, during the rule of Augustus military doctors and architects created the first real hospital in history. But it wasn't for civilians—only for the army.

Since we don't have any Roman records giving the size of the population, we have to answer this question with estimates. The average number of inhabitants in one of the housing blocks (*insula*) can be used as a base figure here, as can the number of inhabitants in palaces and in workplaces. We must then subtract the parks, public buildings, and plazas from the total land covered with buildings. Even the public grain supply gives us useful hints.

> **Did the population of Rome ever reach a million?**

From all of these factors we can conclude that imperial Rome had somewhat less than a million inhabitants—around 700,000 to 800,000. For the ancient world this was an enormous population.

THE AQUEDUCTS were masterpieces of technology. They channeled water from surrounding hills into the cities, spanning rivers and valleys along their course. A precisely calculated slope assured that the water always flowed with the proper speed.

THE ROMAN BATHS (thermae) cost very little to use and were thus open even to simple people. They were often built as a gift of the emperor to his people. Next to the various baths there were also steam rooms with floor and wall heating. People also played sports. There were libraries, gardens, and parks for recreational purposes.

This is the Roman Forum as it appears today. Once the most majestic buildings in the city stood here—and today it is a field of ruins.

The villa rustica was a Roman farmhouse—some were quite modest, others were mansions. This type of dwelling was typical of Roman country life.

The Empire of a Thousand Cities

Tombstone of the legionary Flavoleius, who died in the 1st century AD in Mainz, Germany. The scroll in his hand shows that he was a Roman citizen.

What were Roman colonies?

Egypt under the pharaohs, Classical Greece, and the Roman republic and empire were highly developed cultures. In contrast to earlier, more rural modes of life, life here always included city life.

In these cultures people made the transition from village, hamlet, or farm to life in the city. The first settlement on the Tiber River was the beginning of Roman civilization. As Rome's influence expanded, more Roman cities sprang up.

Wherever the Romans were able to gain a foothold in their provinces, they founded colonies.

A *colonia* was a city outside Rome that nevertheless had the status of being part of Rome—a piece of Rome in distant lands. The citizens of *Colonia Claudia Ara Agrippinensium* (present-day Cologne, Germany) were thus citizens of Rome itself—that is, as long as they were actual citizens of Cologne and not slaves. Another legal status a city might have was the *municipium* (from which we get "municipal"). Over time, however, the differences between *colonia* and *municipium* became insignificant—in the same way that "Commonwealth" of Massachusetts and "State" of California no longer signify anything more than a historical difference.

How large were Roman cities?

The majority of the population in the Roman Empire lived in the country and earned a living from agriculture. Of the estimated 50 to 80 million inhabitants of the Roman Empire in the 1st and 2nd centuries, there were probably only about 10 percent—5 to 8 million—who lived in the 1,300 or so cities in the empire. Most of the cities had only a few thousand inhabitants. Large cities with more than 100,000 inhabitants were rare in the sparsely populated empire. For people back then, Rome, with its estimated population of nearly one million, was an enormous metropolis.

The rural population was not divided into villages in the more recent sense. There was hardly such a thing as a village. People lived and worked in individual farm estates (*villa rustica*). This kind of estate was often as large as some modern farms. The next largest settlement was the rural small town (*vicus*).

Throughout the Roman Empire all Roman cities displayed similar types of buildings. A Roman felt immediately at home in such cities. In the colonies the Romans preferred a grid pattern for their street system. A good example of a colonial city is Timgad, the "Rome of Africa." The solitary ruins still stand today in the Algerian mountains where this city developed at the crossroads of six Roman roads. It includes a triumphal arch, a theater, basilicas, a forum, and a particularly large number of baths, as suited the warm climate.

Every Roman colonial city had a large central plaza (*forum*), a town hall (*curia*), a market and court hall (*basilica*), a meat market (*macel-*

lum), baths (*thermae*), public toilets (*latrina*), water lines (*aquaeductus*), honorary arches, an amphitheater, an open theater, a covered music hall (*odeum*), a playing field (*stadium*), a race course (*circus*), hotels (*mansio*), and large fountains. In addition there were temples and shrines to the gods, the shops of craftsmen and grain merchants, and, outside the city, cemeteries.

FOR THEIR LARGEST BUILDINGS the Romans used a kind of concrete—a mixture of volcanic rock, gravel, lime, and water. It was cheap and easy to work with, and was also very durable.

Rental dwellings in the city in the time of the empire. In the harbor city of Ostia, near Rome, some of these houses still survive today. The ground floor contains shops, the upper floors contain apartments.

The Roman Forum in a 19th-century reconstruction, looking west. At right is the victory column of Duilius, and behind it the triumphal arch for Emperor Septimius Severus. Beyond it, from the right, are the Temple of Concordia, the Temple of Vespasian, and the Temple of Saturn. At left you can see a corner of the Basilica Julia. The long building at the top is the state archive (tabularium). In the upper left background you can see the Temple of Jupiter on the Capitoline Hill.

An elegant residence: the Romans didn't use much furniture. The walls were painted with murals, the floors were decorated with mosaics.

What did a Roman house look like?

Houses in late republican times were poorly constructed and the level of comfort very low. Tenement houses were up to seven stories tall—sometimes even ten stories—and were spread throughout the city. The cheap materials soon became unstable and again and again houses collapsed.

During the empire, however, the Romans developed an architecturally sound tenement house that would have seemed appropriate for a large city even today. We know of good examples of such houses from Ostia near Rome and from Rome itself. The ground floor consisted of shops. Above this were four stories of apartments. The best apartments were on the third floor and had balconies. The top floor was the cheapest but also the most dangerous—servants and slaves lived here.

Elegant Roman houses had a small open courtyard (atrium) in the center of the main building. A small foyer (vestibulum) led into the atrium. Adjoining the atrium was either a garden surrounded by colonnaded aisles (peristylium), or an even larger inner peristyle courtyard. In the center there was often a fountain and the whole was sometimes covered by an ornate roof supported by columns. The walls of the rooms were painted with murals—tapestries were unknown. Furniture was kept to a minimum and generally included only essential items: tables, benches, beds, stools, and foot stools.

People from more northern climates who travel to the Mediterranean often notice that people there spend more of their lives outdoors. There are climatic and also cultural reasons for this. Even on a cold Sunday morning in the win-

A garden surrounded by a colonnaded aisle (peristyle) belonged to a wealthy family's house. On one of the walls you can see the house shrine (lararium).

ter the plaza in front of an Italian church may be full of people. There is a long tradition behind this behavior: after all, the forum was originally the site of political assemblies. At the forum people heard the latest news; here politicians decided matters of war and of peace; and here courts convened and market days were held. Even today the main plaza is often the favorite gathering place for the citizens of an Italian city.

The Romans were very flexible in city politics. In the Eastern Empire they allowed the Greek cities to maintain their identity. People in these cities continued to speak Greek as their first language, in addition to their local languages. In Palestine or Syria, for example, it was common for educated people to speak Greek. Greek was the universally accepted language of trade, somewhat like English in much of today's world. People in Palestine and Syria also spoke Aramaic, a northern Semitic language.

What languages did people speak—besides Latin?

In the province of Africa—present-day Tunisia—Latin tended to obscure the Punic language of the Carthaginians (a Semitic language), but it was never able to suppress it entirely. The tendency was the same in most regions conquered by Rome. We often find information about languages and dialects in the many inscriptions still found today—for example, dedicatory or funerary inscriptions.

In the provinces in the western and northern parts of the empire the Latin-influenced "Romance" languages still survive today: Italian in Italy; French in France and Belgium; French, Italian, and Rhaeto-Romanic in Switzerland; Spanish and Portuguese on the Iberian peninsula; and Rumanian in Rumania. Greek was long the culturally dominant language and even the Romans saw it as the first language. With the decline of Byzantium (the capital of the Eastern Empire), however, and the advance of Arabs and Turks into

what is now Greece, the Greek language gradually lost ground. To the present day Latin has remained the language of science and of many of the Christian churches. Latin has had a very strong influence on the English language. You can see it clearly in words like "medicine," "president," or "subtraction," but Roman words are also at the root of everyday words like "wine" and "cheese."

"I am a Roman citizen" (*civis romanus sum*)—thus a proud Roman identified himself. Citizenship gave a Roman dignity and full rights—with these words he could always claim the right to be treated according to Roman law. In the early Christian movement the Apostle Paul had Roman citizenship. When he was arrested he was therefore able to

How important was citizenship?

A wealthy husband and wife. The man is wearing a white toga over a tunic, the woman is wearing a cloak over a long, full dress.

This funeral relief from the 2nd century AD bears the Greek inscription: "Nardos Chalbos, you who never caused others sorrow, farewell!" Nardos clearly spoke Greek, perhaps Aramaic as well, but not necessarily Latin.

insist that he would be taken to Rome for trial—he was even able to appeal to the emperor. In the end it didn't help, however, and he died a martyr's death in Nero's Rome. In tributary states that didn't practice Roman law, Roman citizens could exempt themselves from the jurisdiction of local courts. As citizens they could always appeal to the courts in the city of Rome.

Rome was generous in granting citizenship to people it conquered. It was granted according to political criteria. In the course of the empire's development, citizenship was granted to more and more people. Above all, it was the army that created new citizens, since soldiers of the support troops (*auxilia*) were granted citizenship after 25 years of service.

Over the 2nd and 3rd centuries, Roman society changed consider-

ably. The army began to intervene in politics and from 193 to 284 AD the army controlled the throne almost without interruption. During this period of crisis, Emperor Caracalla declared all free citizens of the empire Roman citizens and Roman civil (city) law became imperial law.

Soldiers of the auxilia were now citizens from the moment they enlisted. Military discharges, which had once conferred citizenship on a soldier after a long period of service, were now superfluous.

Were there class differences in Rome?

Just because someone was a Roman citizen didn't mean he had political influence. There were strict class distinctions in Rome. Anyone who wanted to pursue a political career in Rome had to find a way to rise into one of the classes of nobles (*ordines honestiores*). The nobility who ruled in the coloniae and municipia (*decuriones*), the equestrian order (*equites*), and the senatorial order (*ordo senatorius*) determined the fate of the empire. Together they formed a thin "upper crust" that was probably no more than one percent of the population of the empire.

The underclasses (*ordines humiliores*)—whether Roman citizens, slaves, or freed slaves—constituted the politically passive majority of the population. During the republic it was common for a senator who wanted to make a career for himself to gather a group of supporters around himself. These supporters—all of them free

This document from the 3rd of January, 240 AD certifies the honorable discharge of horseman Aurelius Bithus from the army. It was created in the tradition of military diplomas, which were originally used to confer Roman citizenship.

Work in stone quarries or in mines was extremely harsh. These quarry workers are driving in the wedges that were used to split blocks of stone.

citizens—called themselves his clients (*clientes*). The senator was their protector (*patronus*). Every morning the senator received his followers in the atrium of his house; he invited them to dine with him and took care of other needs. In exchange he could count on their political support and loyalty.

These iron chains and padlocks, together with shackles for hands and feet, were used on slaves and prisoners of war.

easier. Slaves had no rights, only the obligation to obey. The owner of slaves was, however, obligated to care for them when they became sick or grew old.

In the late republic there were several great slave revolts. Around 134 BC the slaves in Rome rebelled, and slaves in the silver mine of Laurion near Athens rose up in revolt. From 136 to 132 BC agricultural slaves in Sicily rebelled and even formed their own state. In 101 BC they tried a second revolt. A slave named Spartacus organized 70,000 slaves and led them against Rome's army (73–71 BC). Thanks to the trained gladiators among his troops, he was initially successful. The revolt didn't end until 71 BC when Spartacus was defeated by Crassus in southern Italy. One of the reasons that led to the fall of the republic and the formation of the empire under Augustus was the desire for a more stable and orderly government. The emperors kept the division between freemen and slaves, but they attempted to curb the abuse of slaves in order to keep peace between the classes.

Once they were freed, slaves could rise quickly in society. Their children were considered freeborn. Many of these freed slaves became successful merchants and entrepreneurs, and some also achieved success in politics.

This relief from the legion camp at Mainz (1st century AD) shows two shackled German prisoners of war. The sculptor depicted them as if they were already at the slave market, being offered for sale.

What was life like for a Roman slave?

In Roman cities there were many slaves and freed slaves. They didn't have citizenship and thus had no political rights. The slave market flourished in particular in the late republic, during the 2nd and 1st centuries BC. During these years Rome was expanding rapidly and there were many wars. Prisoners of war were generally sold as slaves.

The lot of slaves was usually extremely hard. Anyone who had to do forced labor on one of the immense estates or in the mines of senators or equestrians could consider his life over. House slaves who lived with a family usually had it

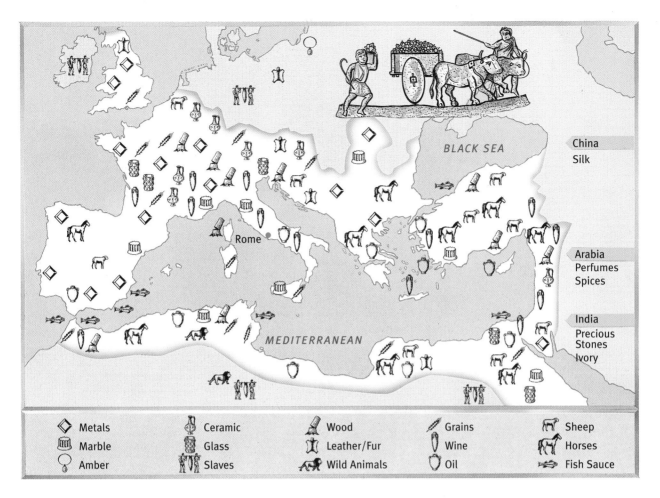

◇ Metals	🏺 Ceramic	🪵 Wood	/ Grains	🐑 Sheep
🏛 Marble	🫙 Glass	👜 Leather/Fur	▽ Wine	🐎 Horses
○ Amber	👥 Slaves	🦁 Wild Animals	▽ Oil	🐟 Fish Sauce

China — Silk

Arabia — Perfumes, Spices

India — Precious Stones, Ivory

BLACK SEA

MEDITERRANEAN

Rome

Commerce and Science

AMPHORAE are two-handled jars that were used for transporting liquids—especially wine and olive oil.

How rich were the provinces?

The various parts of the empire differed from one another significantly. There were provinces that had valuable natural resources—Dacia (present-day Rumania), Spain, and Britain, for example. Here the Romans obtained gold, silver, copper, iron, lead, and tin. For valuable provinces like these Rome was willing to go to war if necessary. The bloody "Punic Wars" between Rome and Carthage weren't just about ruling the Mediterranean but also about controlling sources of important raw materials. Both cities wanted to capture Spain because of its valuable mines.

Olive oil is transferred from storage containers into amphorae.

Some provinces or groups of provinces were economically independent—northern Italy, Gaul (present-day France and Belgium), Egypt, Syria, and western Asia Minor, for example. They had sufficient agriculture, natural resources, and industry to provide for their own needs. Other provinces specialized in specific products and depended on imports for their other needs: southern Spain produced olive oil, North Africa produced olive oil and grain, and Italy produced wine and fruits.

Spanish olive oil was traded throughout the northwestern part of the empire. Archaeologists know this from amphorae found in the region. Amphorae are large two-handled jars made of fired clay that were used to transport olive oil and wine. They were generally reused, but eventually they broke and ended up in garbage dumps. They now convey valuable information to researchers.

Trade with distant provinces was essential to the health of the empire. As long as trade routes remained open, the system of importing specific products from the various provinces worked well. The capital city was dependent on Italy, North Africa, and Asia for grain and other foodstuffs. Whenever storms or pirates prevented supply ships from reaching Rome, however, food shortages became a problem.

The Roman empire wasn't a free trade zone. It was divided into internal duty zones. When merchants took oil from Spain to provinces on the Rhine, they crossed the border between the Spanish and Gallic duty zones and had to pay 2.5 % on the value of the goods. It was expensive, but most provinces depended on foreign sources for certain products—particularly specialty goods.

How did Rome pay for imported goods?

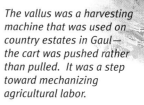

The vallus was a harvesting machine that was used on country estates in Gaul— the cart was pushed rather than pulled. It was a step toward mechanizing agricultural labor.

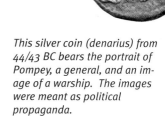

This silver coin (denarius) from 44/43 BC bears the portrait of Pompey, a general, and an image of a warship. The images were meant as political propaganda.

Roman silver from a treasure found in Germany. This beautiful and valuable tableware was probably taken as plunder by Germanic tribes.

Workers harvested crops by hand. Only in Gaul did farmers have any mechanical help: a two-wheeled cart (*vallus*) with a comb that tore off the ears of grain—a primitive, semi-mechanical harvester.

Most foods were available either fresh or not at all—preserved fruits or meats were rare. Wine is naturally preserved and was practically the only drink the Romans knew. The only true preserve was apparently *garum*, a thickened fish sauce

Generally the diet of the Romans consisted of local produce. Imported goods were unusual—except for wine, olive oil, and fish sauces.

WILD ANIMALS for the arena had to be supplied from all corners of the empire and even from beyond its borders. Bears came on ships from Scotland and Ireland, elephants from Africa and India, and lions from Africa.

THE ECONOMY was the basis of many political decisions in ancient Rome—as is often the case today as well. Germania, for example, had neither raw materials nor any other important products to offer, and this was one of the reasons Emperor Tiberius abandoned his attempt to conquer Germania in 16–17 AD.

Germania supplied furs, wigs, and amber. Silk from China, drugs from Arabia, and precious stones from every part of the known world found their way onto Roman markets—and had to be paid for. Rome's trade relations were passive: the Romans imported more than they exported. They paid for exports in standard coin: 1 gold coin (*aureus*) was equal to 25 silver coins (*denarius*). Upper class demands for luxury goods drained the empire of much of its gold reserves. Trajan didn't wage war against Dacia (now Rumania) just because it was a political and military danger. Rome needed control of the gold mines in that region.

Today agriculture is a highly mechanized undertaking, with tractors, harvesters, and trucks. Roman agriculture was manual labor. Harvests were transported in cattle-drawn wagons.

What kinds of food were available in Rome?

produced in the south of Spain and in Morocco. The Romans used it as a seasoning in almost all of their dishes.

The basic foodstuff of the Romans was grain. From it they made a cereal mush that they ate mixed with olive oil and vegetables. There were fruits of all kinds. The rich ate meat in excess; the poor ate it only on festival days. In comparison with our canned goods and prepared foods, however, the average Roman ate a healthy diet.

Even after more than 1,700 years you can still see how well built Roman roads were—this section of a paved road is in Syria.

network of roads like a spider in its web. Roads were originally built to make it easier to move the legions quickly.

Rome's earliest legal code—the Twelve Tables of 450 BC—already contained regulations concerning the building of roads. Roads had to be 8 feet wide in straight sections and 16 feet wide in curves. The law also called for paved roads—using stone, if possible. The surface was slightly higher at the center than at the sides, so that rainwater would run off either side into gutters.

In 313 BC, the censor Claudius—censors oversaw public building projects—built the large road leading southeast from Rome. It eventually ran all the way to Brindisi on the Adriatic coast, opposite Albania. The road was named Via Appia after the given name of its builder—Appius. Parts of this road still exist today! It was the model for all the great paved roads in the Roman Empire. Wherever the Romans extended their empire, they built good roads.

| How were food supplies transported? |

Commercial goods and food products were transported either by land or by water. The extensive system of roads extending throughout the empire was the basis for Rome's highly developed economy. Heavy goods were usually transported by river, on barges that were towed upstream. Alongside navigable rivers the Romans always built towpaths for the humans or animals that pulled the barges. Wagons didn't have springs for suspension and were therefore more likely to break than the barges were. Many things were simply carried on the back of a person or a pack animal. In the desert regions of Africa and Asia merchants used caravans of camels, donkeys, and horses to transport their goods.

Roman roads are proverbial: "all roads lead to Rome." This was true from the 3rd century BC on, at least for Central Italy. Rome lay at the center of this

The Roman road network around 150 AD. Many countries didn't reach a comparable level of development until the 20th century.

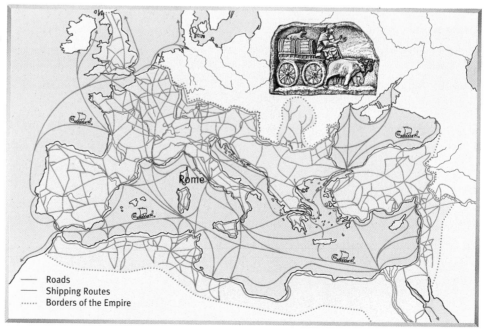

— Roads
— Shipping Routes
····· Borders of the Empire

Road building in the mountains.
Roman engineers and workers (often military troops)
created amazing structures.

INNS after the model of the *mansio* were spread throughout the entire Roman Empire. Here people could spend the night and be safe from robbers. Wagons were usually parked in an inner courtyard that could be locked at night. In a mansio guests could also acquire the services of prostitutes—who were often members of the inn's personnel.

How did travelers cross the Alps?

The Romans preferred straight roads. To avoid curves in mountain passes as well, this often meant building roads with a slope of more than 15 degrees. On such steep sections they used a special grooved pavement, and this provided traction and kept wagons from veering off the road. After all, the braking system on wagons was primitive: the driver used chains or poles to brake the wagon's motion. The many shrines set up along the high passes remind us how dangerous these journeys were. Anyone who crossed the Alps needed the help of the gods.

Traveling in the Alps was restricted to summer. Between fall and spring no one crossed the Alps or Pyrenees. On passes and also in many cities there were lodging places (*mansio*) with stables for wagons and pack animals. Here you could find a bed, food, and sometimes entertainment as well.

It wasn't until the 20th century that European nations extended the Roman network of highways in a consistent manner. Modern societies in the West think much like the Romans: every region of the country needs to be accessible via a well developed highway system. Present-day highways with rest-stops and mileage signs aren't all that different from the transportation routes the Romans developed.

Woodworking was a very important trade in Roman times. Carpenters, furniture makers, and wagon builders always had plenty of work.

Did people travel by ship as well?

If overland roads were difficult to travel, Romans opted for ship travel for long journies—at least during the summer. Anyone who wanted to go from Spain or Syria to Rome tried to board a ship. This wasn't without danger, however, since shipwrecks were not uncommon—this was what happened to the Apostle Paul on his way to Rome. Private travelers had no other choice but to find a merchant ship that would take them on board—and accommodations were not very comfortable. There weren't any passenger ships back then, except for a few ferries.

As a rule common people didn't travel. Those who had to travel were the emperor and his court, merchants and traders, messengers, couriers, administrative officials, and soldiers. Rich Romans were also able to travel, and they often left Rome during the summer and went to their villas on the sea. Educated persons with money even visited the "Seven Wonders"—for example, the pyramids of Giza in Egypt, the Temple of Artemis in Ephesus, or the statue of Zeus in Olympia—a masterpiece by the sculptor Phidias.

Why did the Romans have so few machines?

In the economy of the ancient Romans there was only manual labor in workshops— even if some of them had so many workers that they could practice division of labor as modern

TRAVEL SOUVENIRS were already around in the Roman Empire. Visitors in Ephesus could buy small clay copies of the statue of Artemis in the temple there, for example. The huge lighthouse of Alexandria was depicted on glass drinking vessels. Both of these sites were among the "Seven Wonders" of the ancient world.

This Roman calendar clock found in Salzburg, Austria displays the month, day, and hour. It is a masterpiece of ancient time-keeping.

ASTRONOMICAL KNOWLEDGE was especially important for seafarers. They found their orientation at night by observing the positions of the stars. The oldest preserved celestial globe shows the entire heavens and 48 constellations. You can find a picture of this globe on page 9.

factories do. The craftsmen worked in small shops that also had to serve as sales rooms for their wares. Everything was done by hand—machines were still unknown.

In the 3rd century BC ingenious Greek inventors had constructed various machines, water clocks, calender clocks, and even a rotating steam piston. They were actually close to inventing a steam engine. Why didn't they do so? We don't know for sure, but it seems that a major reason was probably the fact that workers—both slave and free—were cheap. Furthermore, during the 3rd and 2nd centuries BC the Greek-influenced (Hellenistic) kingdoms in Egypt, Syria, and Asia Minor wasted their resources in wars against each other and against Rome. Technical innovations remained a matter for solitary scientists.

Rome's interests were always practical. Taking a small steam engine and develop a functional large-scale version would cost a lot—and they didn't really need such a thing.

To what extent were Romans interested in science?

Medical knowledge, on the other hand, was something they needed—especially in the army. They carefully noted what they learned from Greek physicians and forgot nothing. As a matter of fact, they improved on Greek surgical instruments and built the first hospitals.

In geography Romans tried to uphold the standards of the Greeks, but by the 2nd century AD, some of what the Greeks knew had already been forgotten—for example, South Africa. The geographer and astronomer Eratosthenes had plotted its shape as early as the 3rd century BC. Roman surveyors had levels and compasses, and architects had cranes and block-and-tackle. In the 2nd century AD Claudius Ptolemy published a list of 1,022 fixed stars and 48 constellations.

The Romans exploited raw materials without scruple. Wood was so plentiful they chose it over other resources—like coal and petroleum—for heating and building. Since they knew about petroleum, the Romans could have switched to it, at least partially, as a source of energy. As with the steam engine, however, they didn't see any need to do so. As long as wood was easily available, they gave no thought to anything more difficult to obtain.

Everyday knick-knacks aren't a modern invention. This is a small Roman sundial in the form of a silver ham.

With their sober sense of the practical, Romans quickly focused on the useful side of things. Roman functional structures like aqueducts, baths, bridges, and streets are among the brilliant achievements of antiquity.

Pagans and Christians: the Transformation of Rome

When did Rome become the city of the popes?

All that is left of imperial Rome are ruins, but Christian Rome, the city of the pope, still exists. Here the traditions of antiquity continue into our times.

Rome has always had a special meaning for Christians. The Vatican, the present-day seat of the pope, rests in part on ground once occupied by the Circus where many early Christians died after Nero's great fire (64 AD). The death of the apostles Peter and Paul in 67 AD strengthened Christians' tie to Rome. This tie survived even after Rome ceased to be the city of the emperors—in the 4th century AD. The emperors of late antiquity had their residences closer to the borders of the empire—in Trier, Milano, Ravenna, Saloniki, and Constantinople (Istanbul) in the Byzantine empire.

During the reign of Emperor Constantine (306–337 AD) Christianity became the dominant religion in the empire. In 313 Constantine issued a tolerance edict recognizing it as the state religion. Soon it was the only religion—pagan cults were no longer tolerated.

EMPEROR CONSTANTINE made Christianity the official state religion. A little less than a century later, Emperor Theodosius (392–395 AD) had all pagan temples closed, confiscated the temple treasures, and banned all pagan cults.

Christians were sometimes "thrown to the lions"—or other wild animals. Executions as public entertainment were still practiced in relatively recent times.

This obelisk from Egypt once decorated the Circus where Nero had many Christians killed. The obelisk now stands in front of St. Peter's as a symbol of Christianity's victory.

EMPEROR JULIAN

(361–363 AD)—called Julian the Apostate—attempted to stop the rise of Christianity and return to paganism. The attempt failed. His early death in 363 during a campaign against the Persians marked the end of paganism in Rome.

THE CATACOMBS OF ROME

are an underground system of many miles of passages. In countless niches and chambers they contain the remains of many early Christians. The walls also bear the traces of early murals. During times of persecution the catacombs also served Christians as a hiding place.

Why did the Romans persecute the Christians?

Over the course of their history Romans didn't usually persecute other religions. They had problems with Christians, however. We know some details from letters between Plinius, governor of Bithynia (northwestern Turkey), and Emperor Trajan. When Christians were denounced (turned in by informers) they had to appear before the governor. If they acknowledged the gods of Rome and offered incense and wine to the emperor's statue, they went free. If not, they were prosecuted according to the law.

In other words, Romans would have accepted Christ as a god like any other. But Christians didn't just reject the Roman gods, they also refused to make sacrifices to the emperor—an important part of imperial law. Devotion to the emperor was a key factor in maintaining stability in the empire. Christians were seen as a threat to the existence of the empire.

Why was Christianity so successful?

The world of the Roman gods was populated by a seemingly endless number of divinities. The Romans had adopted many of them from the Greeks. Jupiter was the highest god, and the Romans dedicated the triumphal processions to the Capitoline Hill to him. Still, there was no strict hierarchy among the many gods.

Roman religion was not a true "state religion" like Christianity in the Middle Ages. Ancient Roman religion was, however, an important state matter in the sense that it was a public duty. If the cult and sacrifices were properly performed, the gods were satisfied and favorably disposed toward the state. Roman religion focused solely on this world, this life—and not on an afterlife or afterworld.

Aside from the problems with Christians, bans on religions were infrequent and never lasted long—for example, the banning of Jewish and Egyptian cults in Italy by Tiberius in 19 AD. Under the emperors, salvation religions from the East increasingly characterized religion in Rome. This trend was encouraged by the fact that the

Every Roman house had a shrine (lararium) for the household gods—for the lares, who were friendly guardian spirits.

Olympian gods associated with Jupiter could no longer address the fears and longings of the people. The Egyptian Isis, the Iranian Mithras, and the Greek Dionysus all promised their believers life in an afterworld. Christianity, which began in Judea, belongs in this same group, as an "afterworld" religion. Christianity was the victor. In the end, it displaced all the other cults.

Brief Table of Events

Monarchy

753 BC	Founding of Rome. Triumphal procession of Romulus.
600–510 BC	Etruscan kings rule in Rome.
about 510 BC	Fall of the Roman kings.

Republic

450 BC	Twelve Tables law (first legal code of Rome).
510–264 BC	Early republic. Expansion of Rome over Central Italy. Victory over other tribes in Italy.
264–133 BC	Middle republic. Victories over the Carthaginians, Macedonians, and other peoples. Rome becomes a world power.
133–31 BC	Late republic. Civil wars.
44 BC	Murder of Julius Caesar.

Empire

31 BC–14 AD	Imperial rule (Principate) of Augustus.
14–68	Julian-Claudian imperial dynasty: Tiberius, Caligula, Claudius, Nero.
64	Nero burns Rome.
69–96	Flavian imperial dynasty: Vespasian, Titus, Domitian.
98–117	Trajan
117	The Roman Empire reaches its greatest extent.
117–161	Hadrian and Antoninus Pius. Period of general peace.

161–180	Marcus Aurelius. Beginning of imperial crisis. Plague and invasions.
193–284	Beginning of Late Antiquity. The empire is in a constant state of crisis. "Soldier" emperors.
284–305	Starting with Emperor Diocletian, the Roman Empire becomes an absolute monarchy. He appoints co-emperors.
305–337	Rise and rule of Constantine the Great.
313	Constantine recognizes Christianity.
337–476	Christian Rome of Late Antiquity.
392–395	Theodosius. Christianity wins out as the sole religion of the empire.
395	Division of the empire into Eastern Rome and Western Rome.

Western Empire

410	Under Alarich, the West Goths capture Rome. Defensive battles and retreat from invading Teutons and Huns.
476	Last emperor of Western Rome, Romulus Augustulus, abdicates. End of the ancient Roman Empire in the West. Byzantium (Eastern Rome) preserves the idea of imperial unity.
800	King of the Franks, Charlemagne, restores the Western Empire. Charlemagne crowned emperor in Rome.
962	Otto the First crowned emperor in Rome. Beginning of the Holy Roman Empire of the German Nation, which lasted until 1806.